PUFFIN BOOKS
THE GREAT INDIAN MATHEMATICIANS

Gaurav Tekriwal is the founder and president of the Vedic Maths Forum India. As an educator, Gaurav has been imparting high-speed Vedic Mental Mathematics skills over the past twenty years, to students across the globe. He inspires and informs people, helping them to realize their true potential by introducing them to the world's fastest mental math system called Vedic Mathematics.

Gaurav is the author of *Maths Sutra: The Art of Vedic Speed Calculation* and *Maths Sutras from Around the World: Speed Calculations on Your Fingertips* and his online courses on the topic on Udemy are extremely popular among students and academicians worldwide. Also, through the Vedic Maths Forum India, Gaurav and his team of teachers offer live online classes for students worldwide 24/7.

He has taken the Vedic Maths system to over 5 million students and teachers in India, United States, South Africa, Oman, UAE, Malaysia, Australia and so on. Gaurav is a seven-time TED/TEDx Speaker and has been awarded the Young Visionaries Fellowship by the Ministry of External Affairs, India and was awarded by the governor of West Bengal for his outstanding contribution to the field of Vedic Mathematics. More at www.vedicmathsindia.org

The
$\sqrt{\text{Great}}$
INDIAN
MATHEMATICIANS

15 pioneers who put Indian mathematics on the world map

GAURAV TEKRIWAL

Illustrations by Arnav Chakraborty

PUFFIN BOOKS

An imprint of Penguin Random House

PUFFIN BOOKS

USA | Canada | UK | Ireland | Australia
New Zealand | India | South Africa | China | Singapore

Puffin Books is part of the Penguin Random House group of companies
whose addresses can be found at global.penguinrandomhouse.com

Published by Penguin Random House India Pvt. Ltd
4th Floor, Capital Tower 1, MG Road,
Gurugram 122 002, Haryana, India

First published in Puffin Books by Penguin Random House India 2021

10 9 8 7 6 5 4 3 2

ISBN 9780143446590

Typeset in Cormorant Garamond by Manipal Technologies Limited, Manipal

Printed at Repro India Limited

www.penguin.co.in

CONTENTS

...

CONTENTS

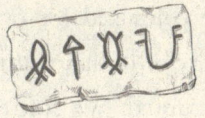

INTRODUCTION

. . .

This book is an attempt to share with our young friends, and some elder ones, the vast contributions made by India's greatest mathematicians over the last 5000 years or so. We begin our journey in the book with the cornerstones of mathematics in the Indus Valley Civilization and go on to realize the true power and potential of India through its persistent efforts and contributions to the world.

The idea for this book came to me a few years back as there was hardly any reference book that celebrated the glory of the Indian mathematicians or even introduced them to young readers. We have played a great role in developing certain outstanding concepts, such as the zero, the decimal system and even calculus (from the Kerala School of mathematics).

With the advent of technology in the information age, we can now ascertain that some mathematical concepts and ideas have their roots in India.

We, as a nation, were colonized for over 200 years and our perception of the history of Indian maths and mathematicians was distorted and corrupted. We started losing faith in our own culture and heritage and started looking at things from a Western standpoint. Many concepts that were widely believed to have originated from the English-speaking world were discovered in India.

For example, the concept of the Pythagoras Theorem was mentioned in Baudhyana's Sulba Sutras much before Pythagoras ever did, the concept of gravity was well understood by Brahmagupta—a thousand years before Newton and the study of infinite series, calculus and trigonometry were talked about by Madhava long before Newton and Leibniz.

I was also inspired by the works of George Gheverghese Joseph, the author of *Indian Mathematics* as I did my research for this book. It is important to now claim our mathematical heritage after hundreds of years of colonization.

It is in the interest of young students that I have kept the concepts simple and succinct; some notable names may have been left out and this may not be an exhaustive list. However, I have tried to squeeze out accessible information through my research, so that it appeals to everyone.

But the list of great Indian mathematicians is increasing even as I write this book. This just in from CNN: 'How a child with a fractured skull grew up to become the 'world's fastest human calculator'. At the mere age of 20, Bhanu Prakash from Hyderabad became the first Asian to win gold at the Mental Calculation World Championship at the Mind Sports Olympiad (MSO) in London.

How cool is that! Another great Indian mathematician keeping the Indian flag flying high!

We have taken liberties to illustrate our mathematicians as there are no credible images to replicate, so please excuse us for any shortcomings on that front.

I personally think what we have here is something unprecedented and unparalleled in the world of mathematics. Included in this book are mathematicians I've come to respect deeply. For example, when I first came to know about Madhava, his research and his rising global stature, my belief and respect for Indian mathematicians was only strengthened. Unfortunately, not many Indians know about him—in his own country of origin!

This also became one of the compelling reasons to write this book in the first place, that is, to introduce our legendary mathematicians to the younger generation.

Overall, I hope you enjoy the book and share with us anything you liked about the book or any feedback (even if it's only two lines)—it would go a long way in supporting and encouraging us.

Happy Reading!

Gaurav Tekriwal

September 2021

gtekriwal@vedicmathsindia.org

www.vedicmathsindia.org

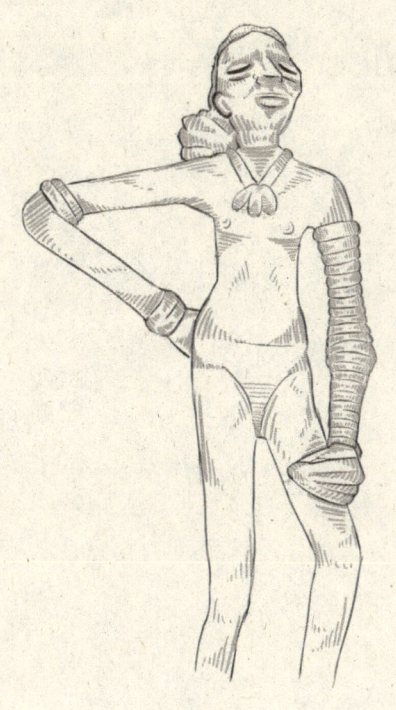

. . .

THE JOURNEY BEGINS

CHAPTER 1

CORNERSTONES OF MATHEMATICS FROM THE INDUS VALLEY

(3000 BCE)

• • •

I was nine when I began studying history at school. I distinctly remember being introduced to the Indus Valley civilization by my teacher, who said, 'Everything began from here.'

Writing this today, I am amazed at the depth of knowledge we have inherited from the mathematicians of the Indus Valley civilization. Not much is known about them as the Indus script has not been deciphered yet (there is prize money of US $10,000 if you want to try decoding it!) but they undoubtedly knew a fair amount of maths. Maybe that is why when I started looking for the origins of great mathematicians, this was the first place I thought to look.

Dating back to around 3000 BCE, the Indus Valley civilization is known to be among the oldest civilization globally. The Indus Valley civilization was spread across a million square kilometres and included over a thousand settlements now spread across India and Pakistan. Surveys, excavations and research done by archaeologists prove that the Indus Valley was a highly organized civilization, which was constructed by intelligent architects with detailed knowledge of engineering and hence, mathematics.

If you were at the site of the Indus Valley excavation, you would find that the city roads intersect with each other perpendicularly (at right angles) like a grid. The houses were made with bricks that maintained the ratio of 4:2:1 for the length, width and height. It is also a well-known fact that there was a standard system of weights and measures in place in the entire civilization. Weights corresponding to ratios of 0.05, 0.1, 0.2, 0.5, 1, 2, 5, 10, 20, 50, 100, 200 and 500 were used. This becomes a fact as the archaeologists discovered many instruments for measurements, including a very accurate decimal ruler, which is also known as the Mohenjo-Daro ruler. This ruler was divided into units corresponding to 1.32 inches and these markings are done with amazing accuracy to within 0.005 of an inch. This length has thus been named the Indus inch.

The Indus Valley citizens also produced unique mathematical designs, like concentric and intersecting triangles and circles. It is also exciting to note the drawings of bullock carts discovered at the site of excavation; the wheels had a metallic band wrapped around the rim. This points to the ratio of the length of the circumference of the circle to its diameter and thus, to the value of pi (π).

The Indus Valley civilization paved way for the Vedic Age around 1500 BCE, which is when we discovered the legends in our Vedas—the ancient Indian scriptures.

CHAPTER 2

THE MATHEMATICAL LEGENDS IN THE VEDIC AGE

(1500–500 BCE)

. . .

The word 'Vedic' comes from the ancient Indian scriptures called the Vedas, and the word 'ganita', meaning 'mathematics' also comes from the Vedic works.

Knowledge during this Vedic period was orally transmitted from one generation to the next and that's why you will notice that the Vedas are rhythmic, easy to memorize and recite. From 1000 BCE onwards, we see a lot of written texts emerge. So, essentially, the collective knowledge is a lot older than what we see dating from 1000 BCE.

One of the many inherent attributes of the Vedic period was the practice of making sacrifices to please the gods. There were rituals that took place at altars, where food or animals were sacrificed. The dimension, shape and precision in the construction of these altars were necessary because the success of the ritual would depend on them. Hence, there were rules to be followed for the construction of these altars. These rules and practices were put together and called the Sulba Sutras. 'Sulba' meaning 'rope' or 'cord' and 'Sutras' meaning the 'process' or 'formulae'. It is interesting to note here that even today, masons in India use a rope or cord for measurement.

Different altars meant different gifts from the gods. For example, anyone who desired to go to heaven would construct the altar in the shape of a falcon. Similarly, a person who wished to destroy existing and future enemies would construct the altar in the shape of a rhombus.

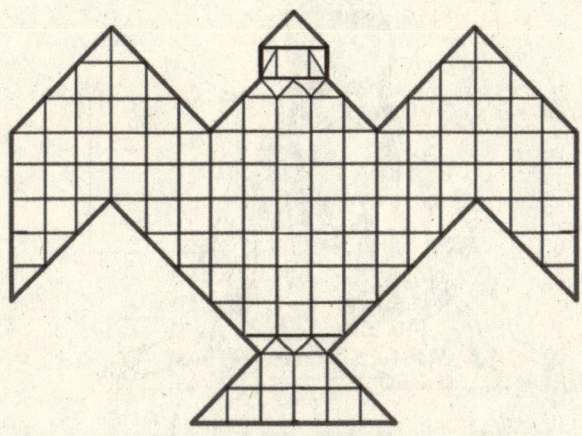

Source: Astronomy of the Vedic Altars by Subhash C. Kak

Out of the many sutras, unfortunately, only nine Sulba Sutras written in the Vedic age survive to this day—those written by Baudhayana, Apastamba, Katyayana and Manava.

THE BAUDHAYANA SULBA SUTRA

Baudhayana was not just a scribe or a mathematician. In fact, he was a priest and a craftsman who would perform a range of tasks, from the construction of the fire altars to guiding influential kings as well as ordinary people on the sacrifices and the kind of altars to construct. He recorded the first Sulba Sutra around 800–400 BCE, but not much is known about his date of birth or death.

He also gave the famous statement associated with the Pythagoras Theorem:

दीर्घचतुरश्रस्याक्षणया रज्जुः पार्श्वमानी तिर्यग् मानी च यत् पृथग् भूते कुरूतस्तदुभयं करोति ॥

'A rope stretched along the length of the diagonal produces an area which the vertical and horizontal sides make together.'

The question may well be asked why the theorem is attributed to Pythagoras and not Baudhayana.

Baudhayana also contributed significantly to the process of finding out the correct square root of 2 up to five decimal places. He also gave various approximate values of pi; according to the Sulba Sutra, Baudhayana's value of pi is 3. Having said that, he used a different approximate value of pi for constructing circular shapes.

PINGALA

The wonders do not end here—let's meet another legendary mathematician who brought us the mathematics we know today!

Coronavirus shook the world in 2020 and 2021, but did you know that the data analysts predicted the number of infections much before the outbreak happened? Wonder how they did it?

Well folks, this was done through the concept of binary expansion. Did you know that Pingala, a trailblazing mathematician, discovered the applications and the processes of binary numbers (where the digits are only 0 and 1) way back in 3rd century BCE?

Pingala is best known for his work *Chandaḥśāstra*, which uses the science of metres in the field of music. And it was during this research that he stumbled upon the concept of binary numbers. In his book *Chandaḥśāstra*, Pingala researched and covered concepts like combinatorics—frequently used in computer science to obtain formulas and estimates in the analysis of algorithms—and even algorithms for quick exponential calculations. Pingala is also credited with a concept that some of you may already be familiar with: the binomial theorem for the index 2, written as $(a+b)^2$.

The *Chandahśāstra* is based on two syllables (long and short) and this is the first known description of a binary system.

I would like to point out here that although Pingala knew binary numbers, he did not know the use of 0 and 1. So he used *laghu* and *guru* rather than 00 and 11 to describe syllables, similar to morse code. Pingala developed different combinations of sequences like the ones shown below:

L = LAGHU   G = GURU

For one syllable:

1	G
2	L

For 2 syllables:

1	G	G
2	L	G
3	G	L
4	L	L

For 3 syllables:

1	G	G	G
2	L	G	G
3	G	L	L
4	G	G	L
5	L	L	G
6	L	G	L
7	G	L	G
8	L	L	L

This is also associated with the Fibonacci sequence, which we will learn about a little later in the book. We will also discuss the contribution of the Fields Medal awardee, Manjul Bhargava.

CHAPTER 3

ARYABHATA

. . .

A period of great achievements and amazing inventions started during the reign of Chandragupta Maurya of the powerful and expansive Mauryan Empire. Counselled by Acharya Chanakya, he patronized the fields of science, engineering, technology, art, literature, logic, mathematics, astronomy, religion and even philosophy. This continued well into the rule of the Gupta Empire, which was when India witnessed its golden age between the 4th and 6th century CE.

For example, it was in this period that the decimal numeral system and the concept of zero were invented. Literary works, such as the *Panchatantra*, were composed, and advancements in science, such as the discovery that Earth was round and rotated on its axis (theorized by observing lunar eclipses), were made. These were some exceptional achievements from this period.

A single name stands out when you look at advancements, growth and progress in science, technology and mathematics during this period and that is Aryabhata.

Aryabhata, born in 476 CE in Kusumpura (present-day Patna, Bihar), was twenty-three when he wrote the famous *Aryabhatiya* in 499 CE. According to Walter Eugene Clark, professor of Sanskrit at Harvard University, it is the earliest preserved Indian mathematical and astronomical text credited to an author. Recognized as one of the first books to emerge from India, *Aryabhatiya* specifically deals with mathematics and has had a profound impact on mathematicians because of its ideas, theories and mathematical conclusions.

Aryabhatiya has four sections: 'Dasagitika-pada' sets out basic definitions and necessary tables; 'Ganita-pada' sets out mathematical computations; 'Kalakriya-pada' is the reckoning of time; and 'Gola-pada' is the section that deals with astronomical concepts.

Aryabhata is often credited with the invention of zero and the decimal-based place value notation system. However, Aryabhata did not use a symbol for zero in his seminal work *Aryabhatiya*. Having said that, the knowledge of zero was clear in Aryabhata's place value system as a place holder for the powers of ten—as has been argued by a contemporary French mathematician, Georges Ifrah.

Aryabhatiya can be considered to be a compilation of works of mathematicians before Aryabhata, along with some works of his own.

It doesn't end here; he covered solutions to trigonometry, arithmetic and geometric progressions, simple, quadratic, simultaneous and even indeterminate equations in *Aryabhatiya*— you name it, it has it. Another significant area of his work lies in methods to solve square roots and cube roots. He also included mensuration, which offered techniques to calculate the area of a triangle, a circle, a trapezium and any plane figure, as well as the volume of a pyramid and sphere.

THE MAN WHO PUT THE 'A' IN ASTRONOMY

Besides mathematics, the statements and results proposed by Aryabhata concerning astronomy are awe-inspiring, given the accuracy of his computations in 499 CE.

The genius astronomer that Aryabhata was, he gave the radius of the earth and the distance of the orbits of the planets from the earth. He also debunked the myth that eclipses were caused because of *Rahu*[1] and explained that eclipses happen because of the shadow of the moon falling on the earth or the shadow of the earth falling on the moon, as the moon itself does not have any light of its own.

Aryabhata even proposed that the Earth was round and rotated on its axis, which causes days and nights. Among his famous contributions are the concept of leap year, total number of days in a year, and even in a week. At the same time, he also gave the correct predictions regarding planetary positions, and to this day, the Hindu calendar, also known as the *Panchang*, is set with the calculations made by him centuries ago. Fascinating, isn't it?

Aryabhata discovered laws of planetary motion in the 5th century, 1000 years before Johannes Kepler and Galileo Galilei!

[1] *Rahu, in Hindu astrology, represents materialism and confusion. It is considered the enemy of the sun and moon.*

In 1979, the International Astronomical Union named a crater on the Moon after Aryabhata—truly written among the stars! On a lighter note, in 2009, the ISRO scientists named a species of bacteria found in the stratosphere after him—*Bacillus aryabhata!* His legendary name is always at the pinnacle of notable mathematicians who made contributions to the field of mathematics and astronomy in India.

SECRETS FROM THE MASTERS

Aryabhata worked on calculating the value of pi (π). You can try this out as well! I quote the master's words translated straight from *Aryabhatiya*:

'Add 4 to 100, multiply by 8 and add 62000. The result is approximately the circumference of a circle, of which the diameter is 20000.'

Clue

This then means that the ratio of the circumference to the diameter is $(4 + 100) \times 8 + 62000/20000 = 62832/20000 = 3.1416$, which is accurate to five significant figures. Isn't that interesting?

CHAPTER 4

BRAHMAGUPTA

. . .

An article in *India Today* made headlines in January 2018 when Vasudev Devnani, the then education minister of Rajasthan, claimed that the Indian mathematician and astronomer Brahmagupta discovered the law of gravity 1000 years before Isaac Newton did. This statement caused quite a stir everywhere, but scholars note that Brahmagupta did have some understanding of gravity.

> A body falls towards the Earth as it is the nature of the Earth to attract bodies just as it is in the nature of the water to flow.

Born in 598 CE, Brahmagupta has been described as *Ganak Chakra Chudamani* (jewel among the circle of mathematicians). Through his seminal work, *Brahma-sphuta-siddhanta*, he was the first to list the rules and properties of zero as a number, and it was these rules that made him shine during the period!

Brahmagupta says:

- When zero is added to a number or subtracted from a number, the number remains unchanged.
- A number multiplied by zero becomes zero.

Brahma-sphuta-siddhanta introduced the Arab world to astronomy before they became acquainted with the results of Ptolemy, the Egyptian astronomer and mathematician. This text was brought to Baghdad by the 8th-century caliph, Abbasid Al-Mansur, and it was an essential link to the upsurge in science and mathematics in the Arab world.

This is not the end of *Brahma-sphuta-siddhanta*, there are more meaningful observations made by the genius Brahmagupta that would stun and excite you!

Brahma-sphuta-siddhanta has twenty-four chapters and a total of 1008 verses in the *Arya* metre. An *Arya* metre is used in Sanskrit, Prakrit and Marathi verses. His discoveries are not given like mathematical equations but like poetry throughout the book— which makes his work one of a kind!

The book is also one of the first mathematical books to provide concrete ideas on positive (fortune) numbers and negative numbers (debt), as we see below:

- A debt minus zero is a debt.
- A fortune minus zero is a fortune.

- Zero minus zero is a zero.
- A debt subtracted from zero is a fortune.
- A fortune subtracted from zero is a debt.
- The product of zero multiplied by a debt or fortune is zero.
- The product of zero multiplied by zero is zero.
- The product or quotient of two fortunes is one fortune.
- The product or quotient of two debts is one fortune.
- The product or quotient of a debt and a fortune is a debt.
- The product or quotient of a fortune and a debt is a debt.

Aren't these notable? These concepts may seem very elementary today, but in Brahmagupta's time, these concepts and results were considered path-breaking and revolutionary!

To see zero as a number was a breakthrough moment in history, which further made many advancements in mathematics and science possible.

Apart from penning down *Brahma-sphuta-siddhanta*, Brahmagupta has also been credited with being the first person to discover the formula for solving quadratic equations—you'll find out more about quadratic equations in the coming chapters.

He even came up with a formula to find the area of any four-sided shape whose corners touch the inside of a circle.

I'm sure some of you have already started coming across these concepts in your coursebooks—well, Brahmagupta made that possible!

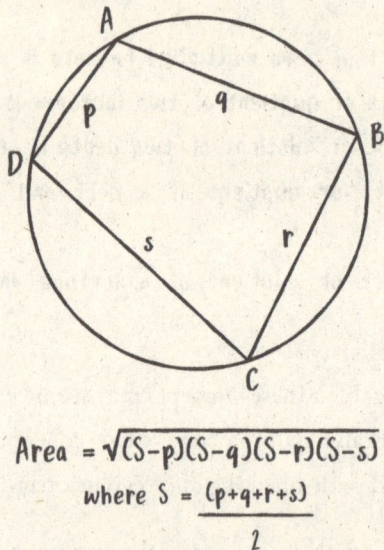

$$\text{Area} = \sqrt{(S-p)(S-q)(S-r)(S-s)}$$
$$\text{where } S = \frac{(p+q+r+s)}{2}$$

This is a commonly applied formula used even today by students and teachers in schools.

Brahmagupta mentioned that the value of pi could be taken simply as 3 for simple calculations and as $\sqrt{10}$ (this equals 3.1622 . . .) for further accuracy. Through his observations, Brahmagupta even pointed out that the length of a year is 365 days, 6 hours 12 minutes and 9 seconds and that the planet Earth is a sphere, with a circumference of around 36,000 kilometres.

We now know that the circumference of Earth is about 40,000 kilometres. Think of how close Brahmagupta got to the accurate calculations all those years ago!

In February 2019, when I met a travelling Australian mathematics historian—Jonathan J. Crabtree—in Kolkata, he was in awe of Brahmagupta's life and his glorious contributions to mathematics. Crabtree mentioned that he is on a mission to bring the student community closer to Brahmagupta's laws. He says in an interview that 'Brahmagupta's powerful set of eighteen laws of mathematics are completely missing from India's current mathematics curriculum. So, I converted Brahmagupta's laws of mathematics into fun games for children. Hopefully, that will help in mitigating the fear of positive and negative numbers.'

Brahmagupta moved to Ujjain as the head of the astronomical observatory, which was also a centre for astronomy and research. In 665 CE, Brahmagupta authored his second book *Khandakhadyaka*, which is a practical handbook of Indian astronomy.

Sitting in the 21st century, I am amazed at how Brahmagupta must have calculated these figures using limited resources, and that too with such high accuracy!

CHAPTER 5

VARAHAMIHIRA

• • •

Let us talk about another renowned name whose incredible findings were one of a kind. Friends, say hello to Varahamihira, who was born in 505 CE in Ujjain to Adityadasa, an astronomer of repute. Varahamihira studied at Kapitthaka. As legend has it, when Varahamihira was young, he met the great mathematician and astronomer, Aryabhata, on a visit to Kusumpura. The meeting inspired Varahamihira so much that he dedicated himself to the study of astronomy and astrology. And what dedication it was!

Thereafter, Varahamihira authored three monumental works: *Pancha-Siddhāntikā*, *Brihat-Samhita* and *Brihat Jataka*.

Pancha-Siddhāntikā, authored by Varahamihira in 575 CE, is the most significant as it gives us information about lost archaic Indian texts and summarizes five astronomical treatises namely the Surya Siddhanta, Romaka Siddhanta, Paulisa Siddhanta, Vasishtha Siddhanta and Paitamaha Siddhanta. These treatises are important as they had widespread applications in the field of

astronomy and even today the system given in the book makes accurate predictions in solar and lunar year computations of the Hindu Calendar, not just in India but also in the Middle East.

VARAHAMIHIRA MAKES NEWS!

Did you know that in September of 2015, NASA (National Aeronautics and Space Administration) announced that it 'Confirms Evidence that Liquid Water flows on Today's Mars'.

But what if I told you that Varahamihira had already predicted this almost 1500 years ago?

And did you also know that in May 2016, it was reported that the solution to drought in India is possible with the help of termites? Ancient Indians knew that these insects could be our saviours in times of drought and that termite mounds are indicators of nearby groundwater. This was also written by Varahamihira in his book *Brihat-Samhita* and was first put into practice by Prof. E.A.V. Prasad from Sri Venkateswara University in Tirupati, Andhra Pradesh.

The *Brihat-Samhita* (authored in 550 CE), which is also Varahamihira's magnum opus, covers a lot of topics that interests everybody, and is relevant to this day. It contains crucial astronomical data, geographical details and covers a range of subjects: architecture, sculpture, medicine, psychology, physiology, physiognomy, botany, zoology, prosody (pattern of rhythm) and figures of speech, among others. Varahamihira made path-breaking contributions to mathematics too—starting with improving the accuracy and precision of Aryabhata's sine table.

Persian traveller and scholar Al-Biruni (973 CE–1050 CE) also quoted specific chapters of the *Brihat-Samhita* in his own work *Kitab ul-Hind (Indica)*. This shows the credibility and scope of Varahamihira's work.

Interestingly, Varahamihira was also interested in recreational maths—the oldest datable 4 by 4 Magic Square is attributed to him. Takao Hayashi, a scholar from Doshisha University, Kyoto, Japan, adds that Varahamihira's 4 by 4 Magic Square, which has sixteen cells, also prescribes how to prepare perfumes from sixteen original substances. The numbers represent the amount of an ingredient to be mixed to generate aromas and fragrances. Varahamihira even developed a version of the modern-day Pascal's triangle, which he used to find the value of the binomial coefficients. He was a polymath, as we can now observe.

2	3	5	8
5	8	2	3
4	1	7	6
7	6	4	1

Varahamihira's magic square (p = 18)

Speaking of Pascal's triangle, several legendary mathematicians have dedicated their time and resources to studying Pascal's triangle. One such genius is Halayudha, who gave the step-by-step construction of the triangle over 600 years before the French mathematician Blaise Pascal. Halayudha gives Pingala (3rd century BCE) credit for this triangle, as he derived it from certain codes and clues found in Pingala's work.

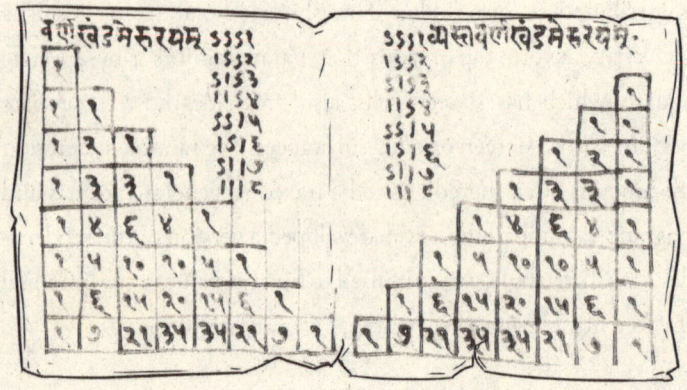

Meru Prastaara as used in Indian manuscripts, derived from Pingala's formulas

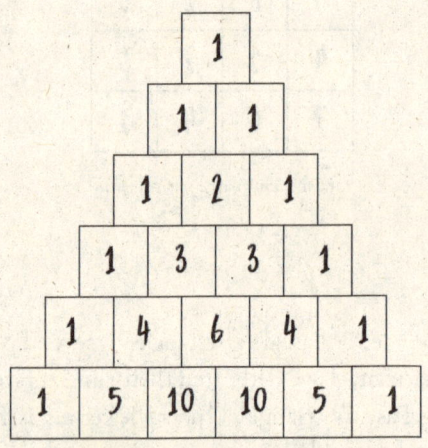

Halayudha's Staircase of Mount Meru

This triangle is essential in the academic world as it is a triangular array of the binomial coefficients. One of the important features of this triangle is that if you take any row and take the **sum of the numbers it is always equal to** 2^n, where n corresponds to the number of the row.

$$1 = 1 = 2^0$$

$$1 + 1 = 2 = 2^1$$

$$1 + 2 + 1 = 4 = 2^2$$

$$1 + 3 + 3 + 1 = 8 = 2^3$$

$$1 + 4 + 6 + 4 + 1 = 16 = 2^4$$

GEM FROM THE INTERNET

There are many other interesting properties, mathematical applications and even secrets of the triangle that can be seen in a TED-Ed Video, beautifully made by Wajdi Mohamed Ratemi. Scan this QR code to watch the TED-Ed video on Pascal's triangle.

SECRETS FROM THE MASTERS

Here's a takeaway for you on Magic Squares. For the sake of this book, we will be solving the 3 by 3 magic square. For a 3 by 3 Magic Square, each row, each column and each diagonal should add up to the same number. You can use the numbers from 1 to 9 only once. Now, can you create a Magic Square based on this information?

The first thing to do is to find the magic number that the rows, columns and diagonals add up to. Let's see how you can find that!

$1 + 2 + 3 + 4 + 5 + 6 + 7 + 8 + 9$ is 45

Each row must add up to 45/3, that is, 15.

So, 15 is the magic number that the rows, columns and diagonals must total up to.

Now, to find the middle number of the magic square, we need to add the two diagonals and the middle column where each totals up to 15. Please note that this is equal to adding the top row, the bottom row and three times the middle number.

So, you can say it is $15 + 15 + m + m + m = 45$.

We now have $3m = 15$, so 'm' or the middle number is clearly 5.

Once you know that the middle number is 5, you know that the opposite numbers add up to 10.

If you think a little deeper, you will note that if the number 9 appears in a row or column, the other numbers must be 2 and 4. The numbers can't be 1 and 5 as 5 is in the middle already. So, 9 has to be in the middle column with 5.

Now that you have cracked this, you can easily figure out all the numbers in the Magic Square.

This is how your 3 by 3 Magic Square will look like in the end:

2	9	4
7	5	3
6	1	8

CHAPTER 6

BHASKARACHARYA

...

To pique your interest further, what if I told you arithmetic problems and algebra can be fun when the problem is expressed in poetic or verse form?

Not many of us are aware of the legacy of Bhaskaracharya and his work *Lilavati*, which tackles arithmetic, algebra and geometry. The mathematical techniques suggested by Bhaskaracharya can be used in day-to-day teaching and his methods hold relevance even today! Weaving beautiful stories and poems into his mathematical problems, he was perhaps one of the first to make arithmetical problems interesting for his students.

Let's look at one such problem:

> 'One-third of a collection of beautiful water lilies was offered to Shiva, one-fifth to Vishnu, one-sixth to Surya, and one-fourth to the Devi. The six that remained were presented to the guru. How many water lilies were there in all?'

See how fascinating 'problems' can be! Are you trying to solve it? Now, let's find out more about Bhaskaracharya.

Born in 1114 CE in Bijapur, in Karnataka, Bhaskaracharya continues to inspire mathematicians across the spectrum. In 2014, over 900 years since his birth, a large gathering of mathematicians and academicians from all over the world gathered to commemorate this event in a conference titled 'Bhaskara 900' in Mumbai.

As the legend goes, the name Lilavati is attributed to Bhaskaracharya's daughter, who as per her horoscope was to remain unmarried. He used all his knowledge of astrology and astronomy to find an auspicious moment for her marriage. He even had a water clock set up to reach the exact moment of her marriage, but Bhaskaracharya's hard work was wasted by Lilavati herself.

Lilavati, a naïve child, could not control her curiosity and wanted to see the water clock. It so happened that a bead from her necklace fell into the water clock and the moment that it was supposed to show went unnoticed. And as fate would have it, Lilavati remained unmarried. Hence, Bhaskaracharya named his epic work after her.

In his book *Lilavati*, the eight mathematical operations—addition, subtraction, multiplication, division, squaring, cubing, extraction of square and cube-roots—are dealt with at the beginning among other methods. Bhaskaracharya then covers ways of inversion, the unitary method, method of elimination, problems leading to quadratic equations, series, rule of three, permutations and combinations and even indeterminate analysis.

The Indian government, in 2015, commissioned a supercomputer to help in weather forecasting. They called the machine 'Bhaskara' as a tribute to his outstanding contribution.

Bhaskaracharya's work is legendary and has therefore attracted many commentaries by mathematicians like Narayana Pandita, Suryadesa, Ganesh Daivajna, Ranganatha and even Kerala School of mathematicians, Sankara Variyar and Mahisamangala Narayana. In fact, *Lilavati* ranks at the top in terms of the number of commentaries it has elicited. This work was translated into Persian by Abul Faizi in 1587 under the instructions of the Mughal Emperor Akbar. His work *Bijaganita* was also translated into Persian by Attah-Ullah-Rushdie in 1634.

Folks, the contributions of Bhaskaracharya in the field of mathematics are immense and unmatchable.

SECRETS FROM THE MASTERS

So let's delve into some problem-solving—the *Lilavati* way! You will notice the author's poetic nature reflecting in these mathematical problems. Can you imagine yourself as a student solving these problems in a *gurukul* thousands of years ago?

Oh! You auspicious girl with enchanting eyes of a fawn, Lilavati, one-third of a collection of beautiful water lilies was offered to Shiva, one-fifth to Vishnu, one-sixth to Surya, and one-fourth to the Devi. The six that remained were presented to the Guru. How many water lilies were there in all?

Let x be the total number of water lilies:

$1/3^*x + 1/5^*x + 1/6^*x + 1/4^*x + 6 = x$

$20/60^*x + 12/60^*x + 10/60^*x + 15/60^*x + 360/60 = x$

$57x + 360 = 60x$

$3x = 360$

X = 120

So, as evident here, *Lilavati* simplified sums using poetry, stories and nature like those of lilies, fawns and gods. This amplified interest among students and helped them remember important concepts, which would have been otherwise drab and boring. Three cheers for Bhaskaracharya for this innovation in mathematics thousands of years ago—something that continues to be relevant in today's digital generation!

CHAPTER 7

NARAYANA PANDITA

• • •

Another mathematician of great significance is Narayana Pandita. Pandita means 'the learned one' and was used to refer to scholars. He was born to Narasimha and it is claimed that he was from north India.

If I were to ask you how many methods of squaring numbers you know, what would you say? One, two or, at the very most, three ways, right?

Well, meet Narayana Pandita, who in his book, *Karmapradipika*, gave seven methods of squaring numbers all the way back in the 14th century! The cool quotient doesn't end here.

Narayana also authored the *Ganita Kaumudi* (Moonlight of Mathematics) in 1356 on mathematical operations. Narayana's style in this book is like Bhaskaracharya's in *Lilavati*, and it is four times the volume of *Lilavati* containing over 475 sutras and 395 examples in fourteen chapters. This work inspired a lot of research in the field of combinatorics.

Narayana also contributed a rule to calculate the approximate value of square roots, mathematical operations with zero, methods for factorization, many rules for geometry and built upon the concepts of Magic Squares. Calculations pertaining to mixtures, the interest of the principal amount, payment in instalments and mathematics related to daily life were also discussed in *Ganita Kaumudi*.

Narayana's rules in geometry include triangles, quadrilaterals, area of a circle, the formation of an integral triangle and cyclic quadrilaterals. His treatise on algebra is called *Bijaganita Vatamsa*, based on a manuscript found in Varanasi.

SECRETS FROM THE MASTERS

I want to share some problems and their unique solutions that can be tried and implemented by you as well. So, my dear reader, I present to you Narayana's method for testing multiplication. This method of 'checking by nines' originated in India and then spread to the world—thanks to Narayana's genius.

1) Oh, friend! 29 multiplied by 17 equals to 493. Is this correct?

Solution rule: Divide each of the multiplier and multiplicand by an optional number. Multiply the resulting remainders and then divide the product by the optional number. If the remainder so obtained is equal to the remainder obtained by dividing the product, it is correct.

Step 1

So, here, the multiplier is 29 and the multiplicand is 17.

Let's use 3 as the optional number (we can choose any number to be the optional number).

Step 2

Dividing 29 by 3 gives us a remainder of 2, and dividing 17 by 3 gives us remainder 2 again.

Step 3

Multiplying the remainders, we get 2 x 2 = 4.

Step 4

Finally, we have 4 divided by 3, which gives us a remainder of 1, which is true as 493 divided by 3 gives us a remainder of 1. So, our multiplication is correct!

We now come to the calculation of areas of triangles or quadrilaterals.

2) **A quadrilateral has sides that measure 4, 7, 10 and 15 units. Find its area.**

Solution rule: In a triangle or a quadrilateral, the product of half the sums of the opposite sides is the gross area. In a triangle, the face (side opposite to the base) is considered to be zero. If a, b, c and d are the sides of a quadrilateral, the rule states that its area is approximately equal to:

$$\left(\frac{a+c}{2}\right) \times \left(\frac{b+d}{2}\right)$$

$$\text{Area} = \left(\frac{a+c}{2}\right) \times \left(\frac{b+d}{2}\right)$$

$$= \frac{4+10}{2} \times \frac{7+15}{2}$$

$$= 7 \times 11$$

So the area is 77 sq units approximately.

Narayana also shared a few problems that attracted global attention. Let's talk about his problem, Narayana's Cows, from his famous treatise *Ganita Kaumudi*.

GEM FROM THE INTERNET

NARAYANA'S COWS

A cow produces one calf every year. Beginning in its fourth year, each calf has one calf at the beginning of each year. How many cows and calves are there altogether after 20 years?

In 1969, this problem inspired musician Tom Johnson to compose *Narayana's Cows*—a famous musical piece. While solving this problem, Tom Johnson came to know about a unique numerical sequence, and a year or so later he found a way to translate this into a musical composition called *Narayana's Cows*.

The solution:

1, 1, 1, 2, 3, 4, 6, 9, 13, 19 . . .

In this sequence, each number is computed by adding the previous number in the sequence and the number two places previous to the number.

For example, if we were to find out the 6th place, it would be the sum of 3 (which is in the fifth place) and 1 (which is in the third place). So we have 3 + 1 = 4. Similarly, if we were to find the 9th place, it would be the sum of 9 (which is in the eight place) and 4 (which is there in the sixth place). So we have 9 + 4 = 13 respectively. In this way, we can find the total number cows and calves in the herd at the end of the desired year.

Tom Johnson translated this into a brilliant composition. You can look it up and listen to it on YouTube. Maths and music are linked so closely, one can safely say that music is very mathematical indeed!

CHAPTER 8

MADHAVA AND THE KERALA SCHOOL

. . .

Madhava is considered the greatest mathematician-astronomer to emerge from medieval India whose works laid the foundation for the Kerala School of Mathematics, which flourished between the late 14th century and the 18th century.

He is believed to be from Sangamagrama, a medieval town in present-day Irinjalakuda in Thrissur district in Kerala. Even though most of his original work does not exist today, Madhava's contribution to the field is best known to us through the lineage of mathematicians that followed him, primarily Nilakantha (1443–1560 CE) and Jyesthadeva (1500–1610 CE).

Madhava made some stellar contributions by using the infinite series approximations for a range of trigonometric functions (including the sine, cosine, tangent and arctangent functions and the value of pi). He made groundbreaking discoveries by moving away from the traditional finite processes of algebra to infinity with its implications on the future development of calculus—a vital tool for measuring time, making almanacs and finding directions at sea.

SO, WHAT IS CALCULUS AND WHY SHOULD YOU KNOW ABOUT IT?

Well, calculus is a branch of mathematics that helps you describe things that change continuously. For example, things change in nature. You may be curious to know how waves move? Or how fast something will fall or even how atoms act. Studying calculus will tell you about the path of the moon around the earth or the path of the earth around the sun. You will find calculus and its applications in astronomy, physics, engineering, economics and even medicine.

The latin word 'calculus' has origins in Rome, where the word meant to keep track in counting in Roman times, and guess what? From 'calculus' comes the word 'calculate'!

Among other things, Madhava showed how the total of one could be reached by infinitely adding fractions like:

$$1 = \frac{1}{2} + \frac{1}{4} + \frac{1}{8} + \frac{1}{16} + \ldots$$

SO, WHAT IS AN 'INFINITE SERIES'?

Infinite series means a series of numbers that are added and are related to each other in some way. For example, the denominators in the series above are all powers of 2.

It is perceived that Newton and Leibniz independently found the methods of calculus by building on and borrowing from the works of mathematicians like Fermat, Taylor, Gregory, Pascal and Bernoulli. But what is not known is that the elements of calculus were already known in Kerala, India, for over 250 years.

The West has now recognized this and accordingly renamed some results regarding the trigonometric series, previously known as the Newton, Gregory and Leibniz series, as the Madhava-Newton, Madhava-Gregory and the Madhava-Leibniz series, respectively.

Madhava was a genius. He went a step ahead and linked the idea of an infinite series with geometry and trigonometry. He even obtained a way to calculate the value of pi correct to 13 decimal places, and this was two centuries before Gottfried Wilhelm Leibniz, a polymath from Germany.

KERALA SCHOOL OF MATHEMATICS AND ASTRONOMY

To create more awareness about the contributions of Madhava and the Kerala School of Mathematics, Madhava Ganitha Kendram—a voluntary association—has been founded in Kerala. The association is trying to turn 'math tourism' into a reality by connecting and protecting the heritage places of Madhava and his disciples, who lived in various places between Periyar and Perar.

They have even instituted an award in honour of Madhava called the *Madhava Ganitha Purasakaram* to attract the youth to mathematics. Mr K. Chandra Hari bagged the Madhava Ganitha Puraskaram in 2020.

Efforts are also on, at a global scale, to promote and recognize the works of Madhava. An emeritus professor at Manchester University in the United Kingdom, George Gheverghese Joseph, through his works, has challenged the status quo and persuaded the West to acknowledge that Madhava had worked on the fundamentals of Calculus.

Listed in the chart below are eleven renowned mathematicians from Kerala, dating from the 14th century to the 19th century.

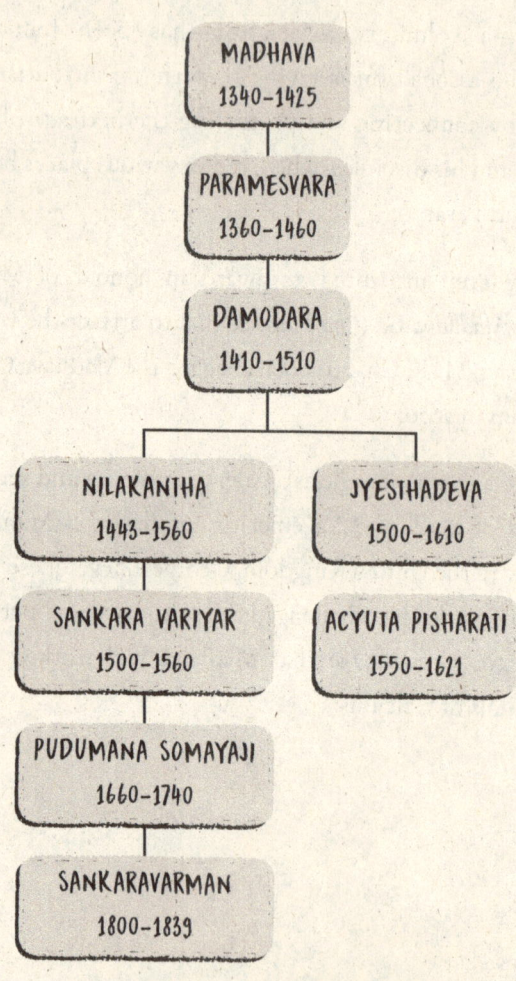

WATCH IT!

- - - - - - - - - - - - - - - -

Prof. Marcus Du Sautoy in the BBC documentary, *The Story of Maths* (2008), shares how Madhava calculated the value of pi using the infinite series and credited him with many 'firsts' in the history of mathematics before European mathematicians like Newton and Leibniz came along.

CHAPTER 9

SRINIVASA RAMANUJAN

. . .

A lot has already been studied, written, talked and even filmed about India's most celebrated legendary mathematician Srinivasa Ramanujan. He has single-handedly inspired countless students to study mathematics and even make a career out of it across the globe with his life and work.

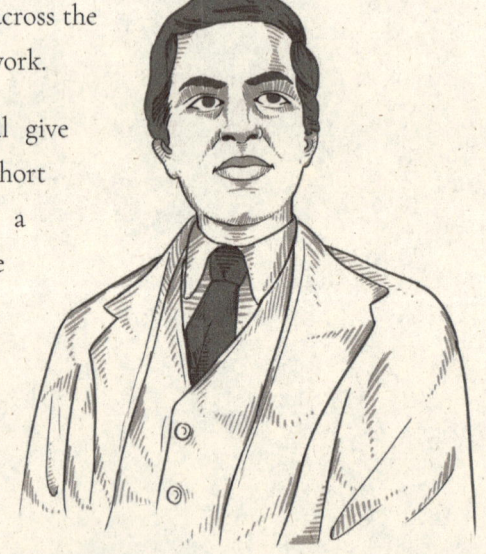

A YouTube search will give us over a hundred short films about him and a quick search on Google will give us numerous articles, essays and books on him in several languages. Such has been the impact of his groundbreaking work.

Born on 22 December 1887 in Erode, Tamil Nadu, his story of becoming a math wizard is nothing short of magical! His father, Kuppuswamy Srinivasa Iyengar, worked as a clerk in a saree shop, and his mother, Komalatammal, taught devotional songs and scriptures like the Ramayana and the Mahabharata to Ramanujan among other things.

When speaking of his enormous contributions, it would be difficult to choose the most significant one!

He made contributions to several topics, including solutions to mathematical problems that were then considered unsolvable. During his short life, Ramanujan independently compiled over 3900 identities and equations, which have all been proved by later mathematicians. This contributed to breakthrough research in mathematics and remarkable discoveries in crystallography and string theory.

It is important to note that Ramanujan's works were completely original. Many of these were highly unconventional, such as the Ramanujan prime, the Ramanujan theta function, partition formulae and mock theta functions. They have opened entire new areas of work and inspired a vast amount of further research. Nearly all his claims have now been proven correct!

22 December is observed as National Mathematics Day to commemorate the achievements of Srinivasa Ramanujan. It was announced in 2011, by the then Prime Minister Manmohan Singh, on Ramanujan's 125th birth anniversary!

Ramanujan began his formal studies in 1892, at the age of five, when he was enrolled in the nearby Kangayan Primary School. In a span of five years, Ramanujan was the first in his district to ace his Tamil, English, mathematics and geography final examinations in primary school. In 1897, Ramanujan was enrolled into the Town Higher Secondary School, where, at the age of eleven, he came face to face with formal mathematics for the first time and then as history tells us—there was no turning back for him.

This period, from 1898 to 1904, was path-breaking for Ramanujan as he dove deep into mathematics. When he was given a copy of *Plane Trigonometry* by S.L. Loney, he not only championed it but also came up with some path-breaking theorems of his own. Throughout his school life, Ramanujan was decorated with scholastic awards and merit certificates in mathematics. He would always finish his mathematics examination in half the given time to the surprise of many, and when he graduated school in 1904, he was awarded the K. Ranganatha Rao prize for mathematics by the school's headmaster.

WATCH IT!

- - - - - - - - - - - - - -

The Man Who Knew Infinity is a unique biopic on Ramanujan's life. Starring Dev Patel as Ramanujan and Jeremy Irons as Prof. Hardy, this movie is based on the book by Robert Kanigel, also titled *The Man Who Knew Infinity*.

The film has been praised by mathematicians and scientists for its accurate mathematics and authentic portrayal of mathematicians.

It is said that Ramanujan was shown how to solve the cubic equations in 1902 and he developed his own way to solve the quartic equation—Ramanujan was a promising student indeed. In 1903, at the age of sixteen, he studied a collection of 5000 theorems by G.S. Carr, and this supposedly became the turning point in his life!

Ramanujan's passion and yearning for mathematics gave him a tough time in the years after he graduated school, so much so that he was starving and living in extreme poverty.

In 1910, Ramanujan met the founder of the Indian Mathematical Society, V. Ramaswami Aiyer, which changed things for Ramanujan for the better. Ramanujan was admitted as a researcher at Madras University, and his reputation began to soar in the academic circles of Madras.

It was also around this time that Ramanujan married Janaki Devi and his pursuit of work started. Apart from tutoring students, Ramanujan also accepted the job of a clerk in Madras Port Trust in 1912. Ramanujan's health also suffered during this period—so much so that he instructed his friends that his notebooks be handed over to various professors after his death.

It was in January 1913 that Ramanujan wrote the famous letter to a English mathematician Prof. G.H. Hardy of Cambridge University with numerous theorems he had researched and worked upon himself. Hardy was initially skeptical of Ramanujan's work assuming that he was a fraud, but soon had to change his mind as he went through the theorems given in the letter. In fact, Hardy was quite impressed with Ramanujan's work on the infinite series and the continued fractions among other things. He finally concluded that Ramanujan was 'a mathematician of the highest quality, a man of altogether exceptional originality and power'. Hardy then immediately made arrangements to invite Ramanujan to Cambridge University from India.

THE HARDY-RAMANUJAN NUMBER

An incident between Hardy and Ramanujan became very popular and gave birth to the Hardy-Ramanujan Number. When Ramanujan was ill, Prof. Hardy went to see him and said that he had ridden in a taxi whose number was 1729, which seemed like a dull number.

$$1729 = 10^3 + 9^3 = 1^3 + 12^3$$

'No,' said Ramanujan, 'it is a very interesting number; it is the smallest number expressible as the sum of two cubes in two different ways: $1729 = 10^3 + 9^3 = 1^3 + 12^3$.'

And as destiny would have it, despite his struggles, Ramanujan reached England to fulfil his life's dream. Ramanujan partnered with Prof. Hardy for about five years in Cambridge, who started studying the notebooks where Ramanujan had listed his theorems and results. Hardy requested Ramanujan to provide proofs and validation to his results, and a part of Ramanujan's work was then published in Cambridge.

In March 1916, Ramanujan was awarded the Bachelor of Science for his outstanding work and research on highly composite numbers. He was elected as a member of the London Mathematical Society in 1917 and the next year, in 1918, Ramanujan was elected as a Fellow of the Royal Society—the youngest ever at thirty-one years of age. He also became the first Indian to be elected a Fellow of Trinity College, Cambridge.

MAKE A TRIP TO THE RAMANUJAN MUSEUM

There is a museum built in Ramanujan's honour in Chennai, where many of his photographs, letters from friends and relatives, among other memorabilia, illustrate his extraordinary legacy that is being kept alive to inspire the next generations of Ramanujans!

Ramanujan returned to India in 1919 with vitamin deficiency and tuberculosis. He died in 1920, at the very young age of thirty-two, leaving behind a rich legacy that was instrumental in putting India on the world map.

AWARDS AND GLORY!

The **SASTRA Ramanujan Prize**, founded by Shanmugha Arts, Science, Technology & Research Academy (SASTRA) located near Kumbakonam, Tamil Nadu, is awarded every year to a young mathematician judged to have done outstanding work in Ramanujan's fields of interest. The age limit for the prize has been set at thirty-two (the age at which Ramanujan died), and the current award is $10,000.

The SASTRA Ramanujan prize for 2020 was awarded to mathematician Shai Evra of Princeton University, U.S., and Hebrew University of Jerusalem, Israel.

The **ICTP Ramanujan Prize for Young Mathematicians from Developing Countries** is a mathematics prize awarded annually by the International Centre for Theoretical Physics, Italy. It was founded in 2004.

The prize was granted to Carolina Araujo, a researcher at the Institute for Pure and Applied Mathematics (IMPA) in Rio de Janeiro, Brazil in 2020.

CHAPTER 10

SRIDHARACHARYA

...

I was first introduced to the quadratic equations when I was in school in Class IX. We were told that the solution to the quadratic equation could be solved by applying the Sridharacharya formula. I always wondered who he was and why his name suddenly popped up among all the European mathematicians in our books.

WHAT ARE QUADRATIC EQUATIONS?

The word 'quadratic' comes from 'quad', which means square. For example, the variable x, that is, squared like x^2. Quadratic equations have applications in everyday life as it is used to find the speed of an object, determine a product's profit in trading and in sports like javelin or shot-put, to calculate the time in which the javelin or the ball hits the ground, among other applications.

A quadratic equation looks like this: $2x^2 - 4x - 2 = 0$, where the variable x has two values.

Sridharacharya was an 8th-century Indian mathematician and philosopher, born in Bhurishresti village in present-day Hooghli in West Bengal. He was the first person to give a formula for solving the quadratic equation among many other significant contributions.

This is the renowned quadratic equation given by Sridharacharya:

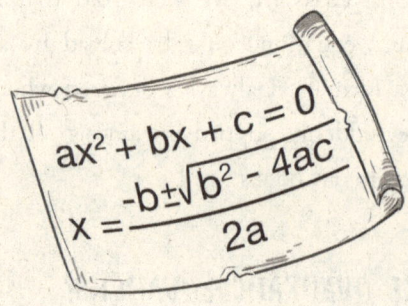

He authored *Patiganita* (means mathematics by means of algorithms) and *Trishatika* (summary of *Patiganita*). 'Tri' means three, and 'Shatika' means hundred. In his book *Trishatika*, he has written 300 verses that cover monetary tables, number theory, the zero, multiplications, division, fractions, squares, cubes, rule of three, interest calculation, business math of joint business or partnership and even mensuration among other things. Many of the concepts, you must be studying already!

Sridharacharya, like Bhramagupta, also presented the laws of zero and he was the first mathematician who wrote about the day-to-day applications of algebra. For example, he wrote about the problems involving ratios, barter, simple interest, mixtures, purchase and sale, rates of travel, wages, and filling of cisterns.

Sridharacharya, in the verses of *Trishatika*, gave the names of powers of 10, which are diligently followed by later mathematicians. It also helped them make many astronomical calculations, such as finding the distance of the moon or the sun from the earth.

Ekam
Dashkam
1 Shatam

A list is given below for your reference. But please note that, in the unique Vedic system, only those names were known and used for such large values like *Pararadahaa* 10^{17}. These numbers were used in the scriptures for calculations of time and distance between objects.

WORD-NUMERAL	DECIMAL EQUIVALENT
Ekam	10^0
Dashkam	10^1
1 Shatam	10^2
1 Shahashram	10^3
10 Dash Shahashram	10^4
Laksha	10^5
Dash Laksha	10^6
Kotihi	10^7
Ayutam	10^9
Niyutam	10^{11}
Kankaram	10^{13}
Vivaram	10^{16}
Pararadahaa	10^{17}

- -

GEM FROM THE INTERNET

So, back in school, this quadratic formula was difficult and daunting to remember. But recently, I found a song on YouTube that helped me memorize the formula and I would love to share it with you. This trick is based on the song *One Thing* by the band One Direction. Scan the QR code below and check it out!

CHAPTER 11

MAHAVIRACHARYA

. . .

'Why to say anything more, whatever is there in the whole three worlds, sentient and inert beings, indeed cannot exist without Mathematics.'

Mahaviracharya, a 9th-century mathematician, had written this in his seminal work *Ganitasarasangraha* (Compendium of the Essence of Mathematics) in 850 CE. He clearly understood the importance of mathematics and dedicated his life to it. In fact, his earliest work focused only on mathematics and not the other aspects like astronomy.

Mahaviracharya, born in Mysore, was from the Digambar Jain community. He enjoyed the patronage of King Amoghavarsha from the Rashtrakuta dynasty and made some significant contributions and observations in this field.

To begin with, Mahaviracharya gave names and definitions for essential concepts in geometry, such as circles and semi-circles, rhombuses and triangles, for which he is admired within the mathematics community as well as outside it. He even gave terms of the power of 10 up to 1024.

LCM (Least Common Multiple) as a concept was introduced in Europe between the 15th and 17th century. Mahaviracharya gave the techniques to find it in his book *Ganitasarasangraha* in the 9th century, 600 years before it was introduced in Europe!

Mahaviracharya also proved some of the theories put forward by Aryabhata and Brahmagupta on zero.

He is known to be the first mathematician to state the formula for combinations. For example, you need to select 11 players in a cricket team from, say, 18 players. Now how would you do that? So you can apply the formula $^{18}C_{11}$.

$^{18}C_{11} = $ = 31824 ways

18! means 18 factorial = 18 x 17 x 16 x 15 x . . . 1

11! = 11 factorial = 11 x 10 x 9 x 8 x 7 . . . x 1

7! = 7 factorial = 7 x 6 x 5 x 4 x 3 x 2 x 1

So choosing a team of 3 people from a group of 10 or selecting 9 oranges from 12 oranges are some examples of problems from combinations.

Mahaviracharya also contributed formulas for obtaining cubes of sums and he was the first person to mention that no real square roots of negative numbers can exist! What is even more fascinating is that it was almost 900 years before French mathematician Augustin Louis Cauchy did so in Europe.

Mahaviracharya studied several arithmetic and geometric series and gave techniques to solve linear, quadratic and higher order equations. He even gave processes to calculate areas and volume.

The contribution by Mahaviracharya is unparalleled and in his honour were created the Mahavira Model School and the Mahavira Award, given to those who do exceptional work in algebra.

GEM FROM THE INTERNET

THE MAHAVIRA WAY!

So here is a problem in combinations that can be solved the Mahavira way!

Say, 6 friends want to play enough games of chess to be sure everyone plays everyone else. How many games will they have to play?

Since chess is played between two players only, from the 6 players in total, only 2 can play at a time:

If we apply Mahavira's formula: $^6C_2$

This becomes $\dfrac{6!}{2!(6-2)!}$

$$= \frac{6 \times 5 \times 4 \times 3 \times 2 \times 1}{(2 \times 1) \times (4 \times 3 \times 2 \times 1)} = 3 \times 5 = 15$$

To know more about combinations, scan the QR Code!

CHAPTER 12

SHAKUNTALA DEVI

. . .

This chapter is a love letter to the lady who made me fall in love with numbers.

I was all but twelve years old in 1991, and I distinctly remember my uncle had got me a book titled *Puzzles to Puzzle You*, authored by Shakuntala Devi, from the Kolkata Book Fair. I was very excited about the new book as, in those days, there was not much playing to do, and I had already read my quota of the *Amar Chitra Katha* comics many times over.

The name Shakuntala Devi is legendary in the world of numbers. Her calculation abilities and feats have inspired countless students globally, including me. She was India's iconic ambassador in the field of mathematics and travelled the world enthralling audiences, including powerful ministers, politicians, business tycoons, sports personalities and even famous movie stars amongst others, with her number-crunching prowess.

Shakuntala Devi had humble beginnings. She was born in 1929 and was found displaying exceptional memorization skills by her father while he was showing her card tricks. She was all but three years old at that point. Her father was a trapeze circus artist and travelled a lot with the circus—which used to be very popular in those days. At six, the young wonder, Shakuntala

Devi started travelling with her father, doing roadshows, including one at the Mysore University, where she displayed her unique calculation abilities of large multiplications, cube roots of huge numbers and even questions related to dates!

Her father moved to London in search of better prospects along with Shakuntala in 1944, when she was about fifteen years old. I believe this was a turning point in her career. She would now tour Europe in the 1950s and later the United States in the 1970s, displaying her exceptional mathematical skills.

Shakuntala Devi began to pave her own way and created a name for herself through her shows, where she would charm everyone with her extraordinary abilities.

At the peak of her career in 1977, Shakuntala Devi cracked the 23rd root of a 201-digit number in 50 seconds at the Southern Methodist University in Dallas, United States. Her answer—54,63,72,891—was confirmed by calculations done at the US Bureau of Standards by the UNIVAC (Universal Automatic Computer) 1101 computer. Even to calculate this using a computer, a particular program had to be written!

In her book *Figuring: The Joy of Numbers*, she explained some amazing mental math methods for the benefit of young students who struggle with numbers, especially calculations.

Soon after the phenomenal show in 1977, on 18 June 1980, at the Imperial College of London, Shakuntala Devi rose to meteoric success and global fame by multiplying two 13-digit numbers—76,86,36,97,74,870 × 24,65,09,97,45,779. She answered correctly—1,89,47,66,81,77,99,54,26,46,27,73,730—in 28 seconds flat!

This event was covered by the Guinness Book of World Records and was published in its 1982 edition. Needless to say, Devi became an overnight sensation and was applauded by the world media, including the press, television and the radio media.

On 4 November 2013, Shakuntala Devi was honoured with a Google Doodle for what would have been her 84th birthday!

I had the opportunity to meet and interact with Shakuntala Devi on multiple occasions, from 2005 till her demise in April, 2013. When I first met her in 2005 and asked her to share some of her techniques, she told me that her skills could not be transferred to anybody. It was Lord Ganesha's gift to her. And truly, she was a prodigy—a genius mathematician!

In the early days of my career, she mentored and shared with me many ideas to promote the concept of Vedic Mathematics globally. She was the only living icon I knew at the time who had put India on the world map when it came to mathematics. There was so much to learn from her. She gave me access to her library at her home in Bangalore when I visited her. To my delight, I found many rare and insightful books on mathematics too.

During my visits to her residence, I noticed that she was a child magnet. She loved children and children adored her equally. She was like their grandmother, and she would bring the wonderous world of mathematics to them. All the children in her apartment complex would happily learn mental calculation strategies and even Sanskrit hymns from Shankuntala Devi, which they would also excitedly recite when a visitor like me dropped in.

WATCH IT!

Indian film actress Vidya Balan played Shakuntala Devi in the biopic of the same name, released in July 2020 and directed by Anu Menon. Do watch it—the charisma of Shakuntala Devi, India's Human-Computer, is unique to her.

Not many people know this, but she had also been supporting a school for the underprivileged to her name in Chamrajpet, Bangalore, for decades. She also founded an education trust to start a pre-university college during the last few years of her life, which sees the light of the day today in HSR Layout in Bangalore.

Shakuntala Devi's contribution to the world of mathematics is immense. She inspires students from every generation to believe in the beauty of mathematics, even today.

I quote her from her book *In the Wonderland of Numbers*, 'As for numbers, they hate nobody, and nobody can afford to hate them!' She continues to give us hope that mathematics can also be fun and exciting and that it is essential to approach it with a spirit of curiosity!

SECRETS FROM THE MASTERS

I tried solving some of the puzzles from her book, see if you can solve it too?

Next door to me live four brothers of different heights. Their average height is 74 inches, and the difference in height amongst the first three men is 2 inches. The difference between the third and fourth man is 6 inches. Can you tell how tall each brother is?

If you solved the above problem correctly, the heights of the four brothers would be 70, 72, 74 and 80 inches. I am sure you had some fun solving this puzzle!

A tip from her book *Figuring: The Joy of Numbers* on division by powers of 2:

To divide by numbers that are powers of 2 (4, 8,16, and so on), you merely have to go on halving the dividend. To divide 8192 by 16, halve once to get 4096 and again to get 2048 and a third time to get 1024 and finally a fourth time to get the answer 512. This technique makes dividing by high powers of 2 easy!

Keep it handy the next time you come across a tricky sum!

CHAPTER 13

SWAMI BHARATI KRISHNA TIRTHAJI

. . .

India, a 5000-year-old civilization, contributed to the world perhaps the most significant mathematical invention—the zero. Through the works of Aryabhata and Brahmagupta, we know and understand that the zero was an idea predating the time when they wrote about it. It is no secret today that the knowledge of our ancestors was passed down orally from one generation to the next. Have you ever wondered how our ancestors did their astronomical and mathematical calculations involving large numbers so quickly and efficiently? The answer lies in a system that is relevant to this day. This system of calculations was lost and was rediscovered by a polymath Indian saint in the early 20th century.

Here's a question for you: can you mentally calculate the product of 98 x 97 in less than five seconds?

This and many other problems you find in mathematics can be quickly solved, and mentally at that; the tricks are penned in Bharati Krishna Tirthaji's, *Vedic Mathematics*. You'll find the solution at the end of the chapter—read on!

The applications of Vedic mathematics are not only for students in schools and colleges but also for aspirants of competitive examinations like SAT and GMAT. Vedic mathematics' applications have also been researched in the field of information technology.

Let me introduce to you all, its founder—Swami Bharati Krishna Tirthaji.

Born on 14 March 1884 in Tinnievelly, Tamil Nadu, Swami Bharati Krishna Tirthaji was known as Venkatraman before he became a saint.

In July 1899, he was awarded the title of 'Saraswati' for all-round proficiency and gifted oratory in Sanskrit by the Sanskrit Association of Madras. He had a brilliant academic record with a Master's (MA) degree in six subjects: Sanskrit, English, history, philosophy, mathematics and science from the Bombay Centre of the American College of Science, Rochester, New York.

He went on to become a lecturer in mathematics and science at Baroda College. Thereafter, he became the principal of National College in Rajahmundry, Andhra Pradesh, India. In 1905, when the freedom movement started in Bengal, Bharati Krishna Tirthaji participated in it, along with Sri Aurobindo Ghosh and Gopal Krishna Gokhale, an ardent nationalist. In those days, Bharati Krishna Tirthaji wrote for several newspapers propagating the freedom movement.

There seemed a distinct urge in him to devote his life in the service of humanity, and he held that man could render such service only after attaining self-realization. Therefore, he proceeded in 1909 to Shringeri Monastery, in south India, to realize it at the feet of Shri Shankaracharya Sri Sachidananda Shivabhinava Narasimha Saraswati.

From 1911 to 1918, Bharati Krishna Tirthaji practised deep meditation and studied metaphysics and the Vedas, which led him to practise an arduous life of a sadhu (saint). He was leading a purely saintly life, living on roots and fruits. His life was continuous 'Sadhana' (meditation); he devoted himself to the study of the Vedas started living in the forest for deep reflection and spiritual attainment.

As the legend goes, Tirthaji, in his solitude, discerned the 'Ganita-sutras' or 'easy mathematical formulas'. Based on this, he compiled the monumental work *Vedic Mathematics*—an original contribution in the field of mathematics and research. Bharati Krishna Tirthaji got the key to Ganita-sutra coded in the Atharva Veda and rediscovered Vedic mathematics with the help of lexicography. He found 'Sixteen Sutras' or word formulas that cover branches of mathematics, like arithmetic, algebra, geometry, trigonometry, etc.

One of the sutras is called 'Vertically and Crosswise'. Through unique applications of this sutra you can actually solve multiplication, division, squares, square roots, etc. 'Vertically and Crosswise' is a pattern that can be extended as well. You will see that I have also shown the application of this very sutra at the end of the chapter. Using this, you can multiply two-digit numbers with other two-digit numbers mentally.

In 1925, he became the head of the Govardhan Matha Monastery in Puri, Orissa, and was the pontiff till 1960—the year of his 'Maha Samadhi' (departure of a self-realized saint from his mortal coil). Because of his spiritual authority over millions of Hindus, the government of India consulted him on policies relating to spiritual rules, temple management, festivals and other similar matters.

Tirthaji in the United States: Featured by *The New York Times*

In 1958, Tirthaji headed the thousand-year-old monastic Shankaracharya Order and was the first of its leaders to visit the West. He went on a three-month tour of the United States and the United Kingdom on an invitation by the Self-Realization Fellowship (SRF) founded by Paramhansa Yogananda (author of *Autobiography of a Yogi*). He spoke at various lectures attended by thousands of students of various universities and organizations, including Stanford University.

He addressed a select group of Caltech graduate students in mathematics at California Institute of Technology.

In his second discourse, he took up algebra and quadratics; and in the third discourse at Caltech, Sri Shankaracharya demonstrated the application of his theories in the field of calculus.

After meeting and interviewing his only living disciple Dr Ram Mohan Tiwari, in 2013, in Bangalore, I found out that the stature of Tirthaji was of a living god. He led such a remarkable life that he came to be known as the Jagadguru—the teacher of the world. Ram Mohan Tiwari considered himself blessed to have met Tirthaji; he owed his very existence to him, his guru.

Tirthaji leaves an impact on you through his work and life. He has clearly transformed my career path and that of many more like me. The fact that I am writing this is a testimony of his greatness and his blessings. I never had the opportunity to meet him, but after studying his work, I can say that he was a visionary; he was far ahead of his time and spread his teachings to the West, making us Indians extremely proud.

In a world where students struggle with mathematics, the ancient wisdom of India is clearly an antidote. The methods presented in his book *Vedic Mathematics* are path-breaking and a gift from India to the world.

SECRETS FROM THE MASTERS

I would like to share a few Tirthaji's multiplication techniques, which makes calculation a child's play.

THE BASE METHOD

Let us take an example: 99 x 97. Here, the base is 100 as both 99 and 97 are near 100. So let us lay it out as shown here:

$$
\begin{array}{r}
99 \\
\times\ 97 \\
\hline
\end{array}
$$

Step 1

99 is less than 100 by 1. So, we write -01 on the right-hand side. Similarly, 97 is less than our base 100 by 3, so we write -03 on the right-hand side. Also note that we write -01 and -03 because of the base, which is 100, and has two zeroes. So, on the right-hand side, there should be two digits.

$$
\begin{array}{c|c}
99 & -01 \\
\times\ 97 & -03 \\
\hline
\end{array}
$$

Step 2

We now cross add or subtract as the sign may be. So here we cross subtract:

99 – 03 or 97 – 01, giving us 96, i.e., our first answer digit.

$$
\begin{array}{c|c}
99 & -01 \\
\times\ 97 & -03 \\
\hline
96 & \\
\end{array}
$$

Step 3

In our final step, we multiply vertically. We multiply -01 and -03, which gives us 03. So, our answer is 9603. It is important to add a zero before 3 because of the placement rule. Since our base is 100, there should be two digits on the right-hand side. So, our answer is 9603.

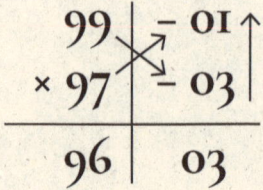

Remember, this method is used to multiply numbers very close to the base of 10, 100, 1000 and so on. This is just a glimpse of how quick mathematics, as shown by Tirthaji, can be!

2-DIGIT WITH 2-DIGIT MULTIPLICATION USING VERTICALLY AND CROSSWISE METHOD

This is a more general method to multiply any two-digit number with another two-digit number.

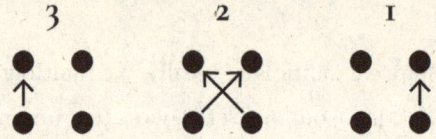

2-Digits Vertically and Crosswise Pattern

In this type of multiplication, we will follow a visual pattern of multiplication, shown by the dots given here. Let us understand it thoroughly.

Say we have to multiply 12 x 43.

Step 1

We first multiply vertically, as shown by the dots in the illustration.

$$\begin{array}{r} 12 \\ \times\ 43 \\ \hline 6 \end{array}$$

We multiply 3 x 2 = 6. We get 6 in the units place.

Step 2

We will now multiply crosswise and add the sums as shown in the figure below.

So here, we multiply (3 x 1) and (4 x 2) = 3 + 8 = 11. We put down 1 in the tens place and carry 1 to the next step.

$$\begin{array}{r} 12 \\ \times\ 43 \\ \hline 16 \\ {\scriptstyle 1} \end{array}$$

Step 3

In this final step, we multiply vertically again, but this time we multiply 4 x 1 = 4. We now add the carry-over 1 with 4, which gives us 5 in the hundreds place. Our complete answer 516. Isn't this simple?

$$
\begin{array}{r}
12 \\
\times\ 43 \\
\hline
5_116
\end{array}
$$

GEM FROM THE INTERNET

Speaking a bit from the heart, the book Vedic Mathematics *by Tirthaji gave me, and countless teachers like me, an identity. Vedic maths encourages creativity in mathematics, which is otherwise seen as a boring subject. I discovered this when I had the honour and privilege to share few of these methods on a global platform like TED in New York City. The students were ecstatic as I shared a glimpse of it through my talk, to further emphasize on the relevance and significance of Vedic mathematics.*

CHAPTER 14

ANAND KUMAR

. . .

'He has done it again!' exclaimed a parent in joy after seeing the entire Super 30 batch get admission in IIT.

'JEE (Advanced) result 2017: It is 30/30 for Anand Kumar's Super 30'—*Hindustan Times*

'In another feat, all 'Super 30' wonders clear JEE-Advanced' —ABP News

Since 2002, Anand Kumar from Patna, in Bihar, has been coaching economically backward students for the Indian Institute of Technology-Joint Entrance Examination (IIT-JEE). This examination was taken by over 11.86 lakh students in 2017, making it the most competitive educational examination on the planet.

Born in a humble family in Patna, Anand studied in Patna High School, a Hindi-medium government school where he developed his love for mathematics. In his quest for excellence in mathematics, Anand submitted papers on number theory, which were published in respected mathematical journals in

the United Kingdom like the
Mathematical Spectrum and *The
Mathematical Gazette*.

In 1994, when Anand was
twenty-one, his sheer
academic brilliance
and hard work got
him admission in the
prestigious Cambridge
University. But as fate
would have it, Anand lost
his father; his family's
financial condition did
not permit him to join
the institution and
the responsibility of running the household fell on Anand's
shoulders. He started selling Indian snacks made by his
mother in his neighbourhood. To support the family, Anand
would also help by training students in mathematics, a subject
he deeply loved and couldn't let go.

The result of this was 'Ramanujan School of Mathematics',
which Anand founded to coach students in mathematics
for engineering entrance exams. He named it after the
greatest mathematician to have lived and contributed to
mathematics—Srinivasa Ramanujan. Because of Anand's

hard work, grit and perseverance, his institute grew from just two students to over five hundred students in a span of three years. But our Mr Kumar was destined for greatness.

Education has the power to change and transform lives, and Anand understood that very well. So, when in the year 2000, a poor student came to him seeking coaching classes for the IIT-JEE, Anand was reminded of his own heartbreak and frustration upon not making it to Cambridge due to his financial condition.

Anand decided that he will not let history repeat itself. He made up his mind to bring a change, and this time it would be a transformational one! This situation motivated Anand to start 'Super 30'.

'Super 30' is a program run by the Ramanujan School of Mathematics, where thirty bright students are selected from economically backward sections of Patna. They are mentored, nurtured and coached for a year to ace the IIT-JEE. All the students are also provided with food, lodging and study material for a year—without having to pay a rupee for it all. All they had to do was focus and prepare for the exam, and all their worries were taken care of.

Imagine what this led to.

From 2002 to 2017, in a span of fifteen years, 391 out of the 450 students of Anand made it to one of the IITs.

Anand's 'Super 30' created history!

He gave hope to those who had none. He gave support when he himself had none. He selflessly turned adversity into an advantage for hundreds of his students without financial support from any government or private agency. Even after the success of Super 30, he received many offers for financial help, but he always refused it as he wanted to sustain the program through his own efforts.

And then there was no looking back for Anand. He has been featured on Discovery Channel and even in the *New York Times* in an article titled 'A Vision of Stars'. Anand spoke about his experiences at various IITs in India, Indian Institute of Management-Ahmedabad and even the Stanford University, among others. 'Super 30' was the 'Best School of Asia' in 2010, according to the *TIME* magazine.

Since then, Anand has been presented with the S. Ramanujan Award by the IRDS in July 2010 and the Maulana Abdul Kalam Azad Shiksha Puraskar by the Bihar government in 2010. Anand Kumar is also one of the pioneering teachers in the world as per the UK-based magazine *Monocle*. Ram Nath Kovind, the President of India, awarded the Rashtriya Bal Kalyan Award to Anand in 2017. He was also awarded the Global Education Award in Dubai in 2018, and the Education Excellence Award 2019 in the United States, awarded by the Foundation for Excellence in Education.

GEM FROM THE INTERNET

A biopic titled *Super 30*, about Anand's life and works, was released in July 2019, starring Hrithik Roshan playing Anand Kumar in the lead role and was directed by Vikas Bahl. The movie also featured students who were in Anand's Super 30. Listen to their heartwarming stories by scanning this code.

SECRETS FROM THE MASTERS

Anand Kumar has made a positive impact on society and it clearly shows in the enthusiasm and aura around him wherever he goes. Countless students and teachers seek his guidance and ask him for tips to succeed, especially IIT hopefuls. I had the opportunity to listen to him one day when he was sharing his success mantras. Here are a few of them—not just for IIT but to succeed in any field where your heart lies:

Practice: You not only need to practise, but you need to do tremendous practice. As a student, you need to focus on the problem at hand and you need to go deep and understand the concept if you want to succeed. Each problem can be solved in many different ways. You need to look out for various ways in which the problem can be solved and then master those solutions.

Self-Study: Anand stresses on the importance of self-study. He goes on to say that there is no need to go to a coaching class for it. If you can take out time to understand concepts on your own, nothing can beat it. Resorting to studying from books, the internet and your friends will ensure success. An important thing is that you try to connect problems to real life and then find out the applications of a particular concept.

Positive attitude: The power of positive thinking cannot be overstated. Positivity will propel you forward and help you achieve the opportunity out there. Keep faith and half the battle is won. Don't be dissuaded by difficult concepts—instead spend time, take help and crack it. Don't make negative statements like 'I can't understand' or 'I can't do it', etc. If you get tired, recharge yourself, find inspiration. Trust me, things will change for the better.

Patience: For a seed to germinate and become a tree—it takes time and patience. So, make room for it. This is a virtue that should be developed for life. So, don't give up when you are unable to understand any particular concept in maths. Persist, persevere, and be patient. The learning is bound to happen for a seat at one of the IITs, but most importantly, a happier life!

CHAPTER 15

MANJUL BHARGAVA

. . .

Professor Manjul Bhargava is the first person of Indian origin to have won the Fields Medal in 2014, which is the mathematics equivalent of the Nobel Prize. It is awarded to recognize outstanding achievement in mathematics. Bhargava received it for his impressive work in number theory. Manjul is the Professor of Mathematics at the Princeton University, and holds professorships at institutes of national importance in India.

Six years ago, when I first heard of Prof. Manjul Bhargava winning the

Fields Medal, I was (and still am) in awe of him as he had the recognition of being the first Indian to do so. He wishes to make mathematics fun and 'less robotic'—which, in fact, is such a cool wish!

In an interview to Prannoy Roy on NDTV, Professor Manjul Bhargava preaches that 'Mathematics is great because there is always one answer, but there are many ways to come to that answer. And in school, we are taught one way to come to that answer, but mathematics is about coming up with your own creative ways to come to that one right answer. There's not one path and everybody has their personal path through which they can discover and that's what makes it fun. That's the adventurous part of mathematics, the creative part of mathematics and we miss that in the way mathematics is taught.'

I concur with his statement because till then, not many mainstream mathematicians had such an opinion of

Manjul Bhargava played a major role in forming the current National Education Policy 2020 of our country, which is being welcomed everywhere. He was also part of an eight-member committee headed by former ISRO chief Krishnaswamy Kasturirangan.

mathematics in India. And the best part about it was that he was taken seriously for it.

GEM FROM THE INTERNET

MANJUL BHARGAVA'S MAGIC TRICK

Manjul enthralls the audience with a magic trick at the Museum of Mathematics also known as MoMath in New York, United States. Scan the code and watch it now!

SECRETS FROM THE MASTERS

Prof. Bhargava sees and beautifully explains a connection between music and maths by explaining the work of Hemachandra, a Jain scholar, poet and mathematician in the year 1150. Hemachandra described what is known as the Fibonacci sequence fifty years before Italian mathematician Fibonacci's book, *Liber Abaci* (1202).

The sequence is 0, 1, 1, 2, 3, 5, 8, 13, 21, 34 . . .

Here, in the sequence, is a series of numbers where a number is the addition of the last two numbers, starting with 0 and 1. This sequence is very important as this pattern is found in nature, in computer sciences, statistics, music and more. It has captivated artists and scientists alike because of its manifold applications.

Let's understand this sequence.

The first term is 0 and the second term is 1. If you note, the third term is 0 + 1 = 1; the fourth term is the sum of the previous two terms, so it is 1 + 1 = 2; the sixth term is 1 + 2 = 3; and the seventh is in the same way 2 + 3 = 5 and so on.

Manjul says, in Sanskrit poetry, there are long and short syllables. The long lasts for two beats and short for one beat. In terms of music, there are two phrases, with one taking twice as long. The long phrase is called guru and the short one is called *laghu*.

Ancient poets studied mathematics just by this simple set up. How many rhythms of, say, 8 beats of short (S) and long (L) syllables, can you come up with? You can have LLLL, or LLSSL, etc. Our ancient poets gave an ingenious way to get the general answer. Write down the numbers 1 and 2. Every subsequent number is obtained by adding the previous two. So, you get a sequence like this: 1, 2, 3, 5, 8, 13, 21, 34, 55 . . .

The nth number gives the total number of rhythms of 'n' beats. The eighth number in the sequence is 34. Thus, for eight beats, there are 34 rhythms of longs and shorts.

Before I leave you to conquer and wonder about mathematics, I also want to quote Prof. Bhargava's statement, from the same interview by Prannoy Roy, on the debate regarding the contributions of India to the world.

He says, 'You know in India I have been seeing lots of debates, "India contributed nothing to science" versus "India contributed everything to science". But the truth is that I would say I have read a lot of mathematics work of India, the truth is India contributed really key ideas to geometry, laid some of the foundations of trigonometry, foundation of calculus was done in India in the Kerala school. So, all the major subjects of mathematics have lots of the key foundations from India, that's the true fact. It's not nothing, it's not everything, but it's really important.'

I think that's what seals it. When you have a celebrated person who was also awarded the Padmabhushan in India speaking about mathematics, you can only listen. It makes me happy to see at least the leaps that Indians are trying hard to make in the world are being recognized.

'A man is great by deeds, not by birth,' says Chanakya (4th century BCE), who was an Indian philosopher, teacher and economist. I thoroughly agree with Chanakya and believe that each of these great Indian mathematicians replicate that.

We've seen this from Pingala to Manjul Bhargava, where each mathematician innovates, evolves and contributes to a bigger concept. This is what makes each one of them a trailblazing **Great Indian Mathematician**. Each one of them has put India on the world map many times over and I express my humble salutations to them all.

THE STORY OF ZERO

. . .

'In the history of culture, the discovery of zero will always stand out as one of the greatest single achievements of the human race.'

—Tobias Dantzig, *Number: The Language of Science*

Before you close the book and head off to explore the magical world of mathematics further, which is of course full of numerous possibilities, here is a bonus chapter to fuel your mathematical appetite. Enjoy!

As an author and advocate of Vedic mathematics, I've been invited to visit and address students in schools across India about great Indian mathematicians and some of their methods of speed computation. I consider it my fortune that through Vedic mathematics, students now find mathematics more accessible and are able to have fun with it.

One such invite saw me quite recently at The Scindia School in Gwalior, Madhya Pradesh. The Scindia School, located atop the magnificent Gwalior Fort, has a rich history going back many centuries.

The Gwalior Fort is known for its architecture and is indeed one of the finest Indian forts. The fort has many inscriptions and monuments within. These inscriptions have been in existence from the beginning of the 6th century. There is also a temple known as Chaturbhuj Temple inside the Gwalior Fort, which has attracted mathematicians and scholars from across the world.

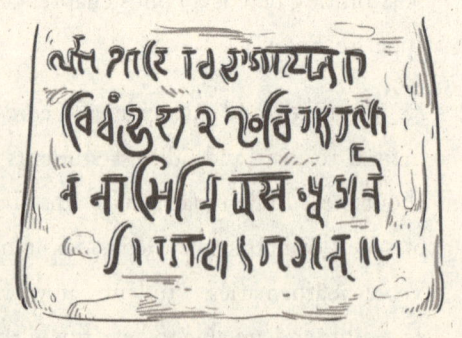

Dedicated to the Hindu god, Vishnu, the temple was carved out of a rock-face in Gwalior Fort. One of the temple's inscriptions contain the earliest known inscription of the symbol 'o', to represent zero in India up until 2017. I was lucky to have seen this zero, which as an idea has revolutionized and changed the world for the better.

The concept of zero allowed us to not only perform the hardest of calculations but also solve equations and invent the computer, among so many other things.

Regarded as one of the greatest innovations of human history, zero is a contribution made by India—something that we, as Indians, are supremely proud of! India is where the concept of zero evolved into a placeholder from the concept of *shunya* or nothingness.

But our story begins in May 1881, in Bakhshali village, near modern day Peshawar, Pakistan. A manuscript with ancient Indian mathematical text in Sanskrit was found by a peasant. This manuscript was carbon-dated in the University of Oxford, United Kingdom, in 2017 and the results left mathematical historians astounded globally.

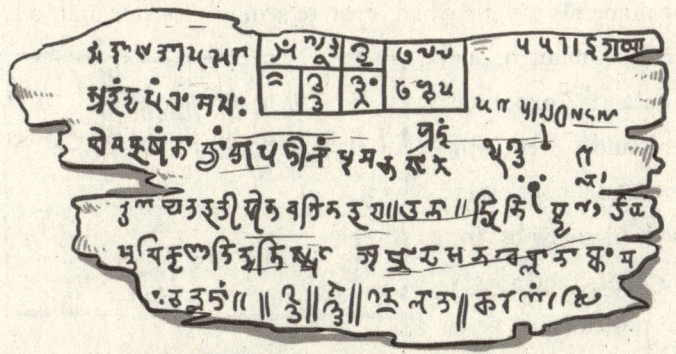

The Bakhshali Manuscript

Known as the Bakhshali Manuscript, it has the oldest known use of the symbol of zero as a black dot. The carbon-dating set the manuscript to be from the 3rd to 4th century (224–383 CE), which makes it older than the zero found in Gwalior Fort.

If you ask me, I believe the discovery of the Bakhshali Manuscript and the carbon-dating results from Oxford in 2017 changed the course of history. An Indian manuscript completely changed the perception of zero from being a placeholder to an actual number.

The origins of zero, as we see now know, goes back centuries ago, even before the beginning of the first civilization and even before there was any sign of literacy and numeracy skills. Zero is an eastern concept, however, the western countries were frightened to accept it in the beginning.

The Egyptians had a symbol for zero and Egyptian numerals were of base 10—the Egyptians had a base 10 system of hieroglyphs for numerals, i.e., they had separate symbols for one unit, one ten, one hundred, one thousand, one ten thousand etc.—by 1770 BCE. But they used hieroglyphs for the digits, and it was not positional.

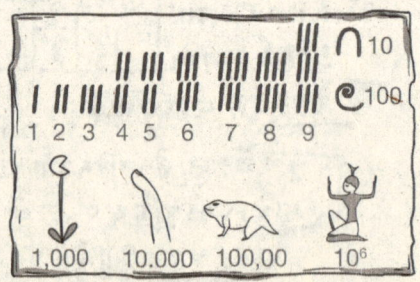

The Egyptian Numerals

The Babylonians had a sophisticated sexagesimal positional system. They had a placeholder zero around 300 BCE, but it was not a true zero because it was neither used alone nor was it used at the end of a number.

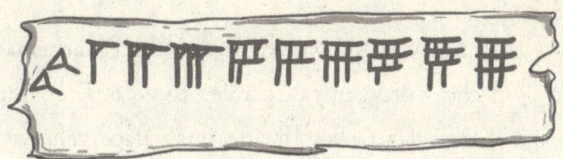

The Babylonian Numerals

The Mayans, in their calendar, required the use of zero as a placeholder within the base 20 positional numeral system. The Mayans used different glyphs as the zero symbol, but this was not very influential. This was around 36 BCE.

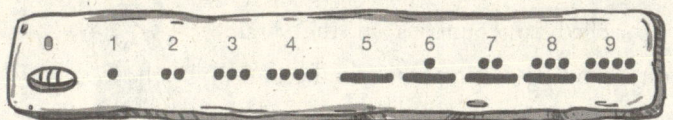

The Mayan Numerals

The ancient Greeks, who had the number philosophy of Pythagoras, Aristotle and Ptolemy, had no symbol or any place for zero. The Greeks were not able to

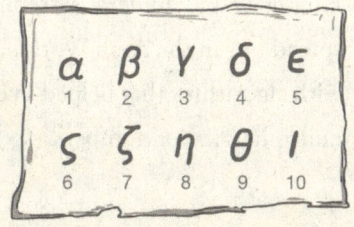

The Greek Numerals

fathom the concept of zero—and the western world couldn't accept it for over 2000 years.

'How can nothing be something?' they thought, and this led to several religious debates and philosophical arguments.

Pingala (3rd century BCE), was the first Indian mathematician to have used the word 'sunya' to refer to zero. Even the Jain manuscript *Lokavibhaga* uses the decimal place value system, including the zero.

Our dear Aryabhata never mentioned the term 'sunya' but he does talk about the decimal place value system. Brahmagupta gave rules governing the zero, as a number, and this is what gave zero its true power.

So, as India built on the concept of zero, it travelled to countries in the Arab World and to China, as zero became instrumental in trade. Al-Khwarizmi (8th century) wrote several books, among which was one about the Hindu-Arabic numeral system. This spread fast in the Arab World, along with algorithms that helped in quick multiplication of numbers.

Zero was adopted too, and they called it '*sifr*'. When the Arabs shared this new number with their western counterparts, they called it the '*cipher*'.

Fibonacci (Leonardo of Pisa), the son of an Italian trader, reintroduced zero to Europe after becoming a mathematician. He learnt mathematics from the Arabs, and he authored the book *Liber Abaci* in 1202, in which he covered the numeral system in depth. It was a rage more so because Italian bankers and traders loved the speed of calculations with zero and hence, it was adopted in all of Europe by the 16th century.

BRAHMAGUPTA'S MISTAKE

Can you tell me what is 1 divided by zero?

Brahmagupta tried to figure out what $0 \div 0$ and $1 \div 0$ were and failed!

But this mistake was rectified because Bhaskaracharya (12th-century Indian mathematician) wrote 'This fraction of which the denominator is a zero, is termed an infinite quantity.'

While the Mayans and Babylonians used a placeholder for zero, it was the dot found in Bakhshali Manuscript and used in ancient Indian mathematics that ultimately evolved into the symbol we know and use today!

The number we use today, zero, is a fruit of an idea sown by India, that later became fundamental to the modern world. This story testifies the deep impressions of India's contribution to mathematics.

I now rest my case. May the force of maths be with you, dear reader!

ACKNOWLEDGEMENTS

. . .

I would like to first thank my publisher Sohini Mitra from Penguin Random House, India, for believing in me and for giving me space and time to complete this book. Without her and her amazing team's (Simran Kaur and Shalini Agrawal) support and encouragement, this book would perhaps never have seen the light of the day.

I would like to thank Arnav Chakraborty, who has designed the book with his well-thought-out illustrations and sketches. He put in a lot of thought into designing the look and feel of each mathematician included in the book. I am thankful to him for his splendid work.

I would like to thank my wife, Shree, for her unflinching support and leading our office: Vedic Maths Forum India. She took control, so I could research and write the book over the last two years. She also took care of the powerhouse—our seven-year-old, Miraaya.

I would like to thank my parents, who have encouraged and supported me through the ups and downs of life. I would consider myself happy if I've done them proud in the smallest of ways—through my work or otherwise.

I would like to thank the readers of my books and participants of my online courses and masterclasses. Your support in the form of emails and WhatsApp messages mean the world to me. You guys are my lifeline, and every single day when I open my inbox, I'm grateful for your love.

I would also like to thank my entire team at Vedic Maths Forum India, who share the concepts of Vedic mathematics with students and teachers worldwide live, every single day and round the clock. I am grateful to you guys for sharing my passion of Vedic mathematics with the world and I hope this team grows manifold with your positive energy.

The National Education Policy 2020 is out, and I would like to welcome it with open arms as it aims to develop India into a global leader in the field of knowledge. With the blessing of God, I hope this book resonates with the Gen X, the Millennials, the Zoomers and Generation Alpha and wish that we add many more names to this book soon. Thank you so very much!

Thanks also to the great teachers who shaped my career . . .

MY MENTORS, 2005

With Shakuntala Devi

With the current Shankaracharya of Puri

BIBLIOGRAPHY

. . .

Chapter 1. Cornerstones of Mathematics in the Indus Valley (3000 BCE)

- Joseph, George Gheverghese. *The Crest of the Peacock*. New Jersey: Princeton University Press, 2011

Chapter 2. The Mathematical Legends in the Vedic Age (1500–500 BCE)

- Shrivastava, Preet, and Mahesh Sharma. *Bharat Ke Mahan Ganitagya* [India's Great Mathematicians]. New Delhi: Prabhat Prakashan, 2019

Chapter 3. Aryabhata

- Clark, Walter Eugene. *The Aryabhatiya of Aryabhata*. Delhi: D.K. Printworld, 2015

- PTI. 'Indian scientists discover new bacteria in Stratosphere'. last modified 16 March 2009. https://timesofindia.

indiatimes.com/home/science/Indian-scientists-discover-new-bacteria-in-Stratosphere/articleshow/4272685.cms

Chapter 4. Brahmagupta

- TNN. 'Brahmagupta-II, not Isaac Newton, discovered gravity: Rajasthan Education Minister'. last modified 10 January 2018. https://timesofindia.indiatimes.com/india/a-bid-to-change-history-of-gravity-as-we-know-it/articleshow/62436479.cms

- B.E. Bureau. 'Brahmagupta's 18 laws of mathematics are completely missing from India's present mathematics curriculum'. last modified 30 November 2018. https://businesseconomics.in/%E2%80%9Cbrahmagupta%E2%80%99s-18-laws-mathematics-are-completely-missing-india%E2%80%99s-present-mathematics-curriculum%E2%80%9D

Chapter 5. Varahamihira

- Indo-Asian News Service. 'Solution to Drought Possible with the Help of Termites: Study'. last modified 8 May 2016. https://www.ndtv.com/india-news/solution-to-drought-possible-with-the-help-of-termites-study-1404026

Chapter 6. Bhaskaracharya

- Sudhakar Agarkar. 'A Brief Report on Bhaskara900'. http://www.vpmthane.org/bhaskara900/

- PTI. 'Supercomputer "Bhaskara" unveiled, to help better weather forecast', last modified 2 June 2015. https://economictimes.indiatimes.com/news/science/supercomputer-bhaskara-unveiled-to-help-better-weather-forecast/articleshow/47518753.cms?utm_source=contentofinterest&utm_medium=text&utm_campaign=cppst

Chapter 7. Narayana Pandita

- 'Tom Johnson, Illustrated Music #8, Narayana's Cows'. YouTube video. 13:30. posted by 'Tom Johnson'. 21 July 2018. https://www.youtube.com/watch?v=VOS3piSMS9E

- 'Vedic Math—A new perspective of Mathematics|Gaurav Tekriwal|TEDxYouth@LMGC'. YouTube video. 13:56. posted by 'TEDx Talks'. 18 September 2019. https://www.youtube.com/watch?v=PTMIxQ53MOM

Chapter 8. Madhava and the Kerela School

- Joseph, George Gheverghese. *Indian Mathematics: Engaging with the World from Ancient to Modern Times*. New Delhi: Speaking Tiger Publishers, 2016

- Madhava Mathematics Competition. www.madhavacompetition.in

- 'Madhava of Sangamagrama'. *Wikipedia.* last modified 4 June 2021. https://en.wikipedia.org/wiki/Madhava_of_Sangamagrama

- Steward, Ian. *Significant Figures: Lives and Works of Trailblazing Mathematicians.* London: Profile Books, 2017

Chapter 9. Srinivasa Ramanujan

- Kanigel, Robert. *The Man Who Knew Infinity: A Life of the Genius Ramanujan.* London: Abacus, 1992

- Srinivasa Ramanujan Centre. https://sas.sastra.edu/ramanujan/index.php

Chapter 10. Sridharacharya

- Heroor, Venugopal D. *The History of Mathematics and Mathematicians of India.* Karnataka: Vidya Bharati Karnataka, 2016.

Chapter 11. Mahaviracharya

- Verma, Devi Prasad, Shriram Chauthaiwale, and Devendra Rao Deshmukh. *Eminent Mathematicians of Bharat* 2019

Chapter 12. Shakuntala Devi

- Devi, Shakuntala. *In the Wonderland of Numbers: Maths and Your Child.* New Delhi: Orient Paperbacks, 2006

Chapter 13. His Holiness Swami Bharati Krishna Tirthaji

- Jagadguru Swami Sri Bharati Krishna Tirthaji Maharaja. *Vedic Mathematics*. Delhi: Motilal Banarsidass, 1965

- Tekriwal, Gaurav. *Maths Sutra: The Art of Vedic Speed Calculation*. Gurgaon: Penguin Random House India, 2015

Chapter 14. Anand Kumar

- Kumar, Anand. *Super 30: Changing the World 30 Students at a Time*. Gurgaon: Penguin Random House India, 2016

Chapter 15. Manjul Bhargava

- 'India Questions math genius Professor Manjul Bhargava'. YouTube video. 20:48. posted by 'NDTV'. 21 January 2015. https://www.youtube.com/watch?v=2MCK3eVwTw4

The Story of Zero

- Seife, Charles. *Zero: The Biography of a Dangerous Idea*. USA: Penguin Books, 2000

- Aczel, Amir D. Finding *Zero: A Mathematician's Odyssey to Uncover Origins of Numbers*. USA: Pan Macmillan, 2015

Maths Sutras from Around the World: Speed Calculations on Your Fingertips

Have no fear as your super cool maths companion is here! Learn how to be quick and better at maths with this well-researched book that has an amazing collection of mathematical techniques from around the world. Use these sutras along with the activity sheets to master the secret know-hows and achieve exceptional results. Explore ingenious maths concepts and systems, and try your hand at popular puzzles like KenKen, Kakuro and Alphametics. Who says maths can't be fun?

It's time to compute like a boss!

Let's Do This Together: Maths Stories to Solve
Lubaina Bandukwala and Vineeta Kanoria

How much? How many? How far? How small?

Maths helps make sense of the world around us. How many mangoes are needed to make a jar of pickle? How many toes do the monsters under the bed have? How many days till the new moon?

Let's Do This Together is filled with stories that cleverly weave everyday maths problems into the narrative so children can easily solve them with the help of a parent, teacher or friend.

As they start with sums that are easy-peasy, move to mostly easy and then to ones that are not that easy, the book helps them build their self-confidence and number proficiency.

NOTES

. . .

NOTES

...

_____

_____

_____

_____

_____

_____

_____

_____

_____

_____

_____

_____

_____

_____